CU00944246

contents

Please note that Australian cup and spoon measurements are metric.
A conversion chart appears on page 62.

about the wok

Stir-frying is one of the healthiest and quickest
ways to cook. You don't need a wok to do it, but it
does make the job easier. You don't have to spend a
lot of money on a wok – the best ones are made from
cast iron and can be bought cheaply at Chinese
food stores. Don't buy a wok with a non-stick lining
because these are not suitable for cooking over
high heat – and high heat is exactly what
you need when you're stir-frying.

A new wok needs to be seasoned. This simply means it must be heated several times to make the surface clean and slippery. To season a wok, pour in 2 tablespoons of cooking oil and wipe the entire surface with it, using absorbent paper. Heat the wok slowly for 10 to 15 minutes then wipe thoroughly with more absorbent paper, which will become black. Repeat several times until the paper wipes clean.

A wok chan is a helpful utensil when stir-frying – it's a small shovel-like implement with a curved blade that fits the curve of the wok. You can buy them at Chinese food stores. Its disadvantage is that the steel-on-steel scraping noise is a bit irksome. If this bothers you, use a wooden spoon.

Tips on stir-frying

• If you have an exhaust fan, turn it on high. Otherwise open windows and doors.

• Have all the ingredients prepared, measured and immediately at hand. The food should be cut into small, uniform pieces.

• Heat the wok until it is very hot before adding the oil, then heat the oil until it is just starting to smoke before adding any food.

• Keep the food moving constantly using a wok chan or wooden spoon. The idea is that the food at the bottom of the wok, where the heat is most intense, sears, before being instantly moved around the side of the wok to be replaced by more pieces. One hand should hold the wok while the other holds the chan or spoon, and they should work together, tilting and moving the wok while tossing and stirring. The entire process should take only minutes.

seafood

swordfish and scallops

2 tablespoons peanut oil
350g swordfish steak, cut into strips
300g scallops, without roe
2 cloves garlic, crushed
4cm piece fresh ginger (20g), grated
2 medium carrots (240g), cut into matchsticks
2 shallots (50g), sliced thinly
227g can water chestnuts, rinsed, halved
1 small red capsicum (150g), sliced thinly
2 tablespoons water
1 tablespoon oyster sauce
1 tablespoon light soy sauce
1 tablespoon sweet chilli sauce
2 teaspoons golden syrup
150g snow peas, trimmed, sliced diagonally

1 Heat half the oil in wok; stir-fry fish until browned. Remove from wok.
2 Add scallops, garlic and ginger to wok; stir-fry until scallops change in colour. Remove from wok.
3 Heat remaining oil in wok; stir-fry carrot and shallot until browned. Add chestnuts, capsicum, the water, sauces and syrup to wok; stir-fry until mixture thickens slightly.
4 Return seafood to wok with snow peas; stir-fry until just tender.

preparation time 20 minutes
cooking time 10 minutes
serves 4
nutritional count per serving 12.3g total fat (2.5g saturated fat); 1258kJ (301 cal); 15.6g carbohydrate; 29.7g protein; 4.6g fibre
tip You can use any firm white fish fillets you like in this recipe.

chilli squid salad

3 cleaned squid hoods (450g)
1 tablespoon sweet chilli sauce
2 teaspoons fish sauce
2 teaspoons lime juice
1 tablespoon peanut oil
1 telegraph cucumber (400g), halved lengthways, sliced thinly
3 green onions, sliced thinly
1 cup (80g) bean sprouts
¼ cup firmly packed fresh coriander leaves
⅓ cup firmly packed fresh mint leaves
1 fresh long red chilli, sliced thinly
¼ cup (60ml) sweet chilli sauce, extra
1 tablespoon lime juice, extra

1 Cut squid hoods in half lengthways; score inside in a diagonal pattern. Cut each half in four pieces.
2 Combine squid, sauces and juice in medium bowl.
3 Heat oil in wok; stir-fry squid, in batches, until cooked through.
4 Combine squid in large bowl with remaining ingredients.

preparation time 15 minutes
cooking time 10 minutes
serves 4
nutritional count per serving 6.6g total fat (1.4g saturated fat); 744kJ (178 cal); 6.5g carbohydrate; 21.4g protein; 3g fibre

spiced coconut prawn stir-fry

1.3kg uncooked medium king prawns
500g cauliflower, cut into florets
200g broccoli, cut into florets
1 medium brown onion (150g), sliced thinly
2 cloves garlic, sliced thinly
2 fresh long red chillies, sliced thinly
1 teaspoon ground turmeric
2 teaspoons yellow mustard seeds
¼ teaspoon ground cardamom
½ teaspoon ground cumin
140ml can coconut milk
2 tablespoons mango chutney

1 Shell and devein prawns, leaving tails intact. Combine prawns and remaining ingredients in large bowl.
2 Stir-fry ingredients in heated oiled wok until vegetables are just tender.

preparation time 10 minutes
cooking time 10 minutes
serves 4
nutritional count per serving 8.7g total fat (6.5g saturated fat); 1225kJ (293 cal); 11.9g carbohydrate; 38.5g protein; 6g fibre
tip Serve with steamed jasmine rice, if you like.

sweet chilli plum chicken with noodles

¼ cup (60ml) sweet chilli sauce
2 tablespoons plum sauce
750g chicken thigh fillets, sliced thinly
450g hokkien noodles
227g can water chestnuts, rinsed, halved
8 green onions, sliced thickly
1 fresh long red chilli, sliced thinly
2 cloves garlic, crushed
300g buk choy, trimmed, chopped coarsely

1   Combine sauces with chicken in large bowl. Cover; refrigerate 1 hour.
2   Heat oiled wok; stir-fry chicken mixture, in batches, until browned.
3   Meanwhile, place noodles in medium heatproof bowl, cover with boiling water; separate with fork, drain.
4   Stir-fry chestnuts, onion, chilli and garlic in wok 2 minutes. Return chicken to wok with buk choy; stir-fry until chicken is cooked through. Serve with noodles.

preparation time 20 minutes (plus refrigeration time)
cooking time 20 minutes
serves 4
nutritional count per serving 14.9g total fat (4.2g saturated fat); 2011kJ (481 cal); 43.1g carbohydrate; 41g protein; 5.4g fibre

ginger-plum chicken and noodle stir-fry

450g hokkien noodles
2 tablespoons vegetable oil
600g chicken breast fillets, sliced thinly
1 medium brown onion (150g), sliced thinly
1 clove garlic, crushed
3cm piece fresh ginger (15g), grated
400g packaged fresh asian stir-fry vegetables
2 tablespoons sweet chilli sauce
2 tablespoons plum sauce

1   Place noodles in medium heatproof bowl, cover with boiling water; separate with fork, drain.
2   Heat half the oil in wok; stir-fry chicken, in batches, until browned.
3   Heat remaining oil in wok; stir-fry onion, garlic and ginger until onion softens. Add vegetables; stir-fry until just tender. Return chicken to wok with noodles and sauces; stir-fry until hot.

preparation time 15 minutes
cooking time 15 minutes
serves 4
nutritional count per serving 19.4g total fat (4.6g saturated fat); 2784kJ (666 cal); 73.3g carbohydrate; 45.6g protein; 6.2g fibre
tip We used a 400g packet of prepared asian stir-fry vegetables for this recipe, available from supermarkets.

chicken sang choy bow

1 tablespoon peanut oil
1 fresh long red chilli,
    chopped finely
2 cloves garlic, crushed
400g chicken mince
1 small red capsicum (150g),
    chopped finely
⅓ cup (80ml) lemon juice
½ cup (80g) blanched
    almonds, toasted,
        chopped finely
½ cup finely chopped
    fresh basil
2 tablespoons kecap manis
1 cup (80g) bean sprouts
100g crisp fried noodles
12 large iceberg lettuce leaves

1   Heat oil in wok; stir-fry chilli and garlic until fragrant. Add mince and capsicum; stir-fry until mince is cooked through.
2   Add juice, nuts, basil, kecap manis and sprouts to wok; stir-fry 1 minute. Stir in half the noodles.
3   Divide sang choy bow among lettuce leaves; serve sprinkled with remaining noodles.

preparation time 10 minutes
cooking time 15 minutes
serves 4
nutritional count per serving 25.1g total fat (4.2g saturated fat); 1735kJ (415 cal); 16.2g carbohydrate; 28.3g protein; 5g fibre
tip Fried noodles are sold in 100g packets in supermarkets and Asian food stores.

mixed mushrooms and chicken with crispy noodles

1 tablespoon peanut oil
1kg chicken thigh fillets, sliced thinly
2 cloves garlic, crushed
8 green onions, chopped coarsely
200g fresh shiitake mushrooms, chopped coarsely
200g gai lan, chopped coarsely
100g oyster mushrooms, chopped coarsely
⅓ cup (80ml) vegetarian mushroom oyster sauce
100g enoki mushrooms
50g fried noodles

1 Heat oil in wok; stir-fry chicken, in batches, until cooked.
2 Return chicken to wok with garlic and onion; stir-fry until onion softens. Add shiitake mushrooms; stir-fry until tender. Add gai lan, oyster mushrooms and sauce; stir-fry until vegetables are tender.
3 Remove from heat; toss through enoki mushrooms and noodles.

preparation time 15 minutes
cooking time 20 minutes
serves 4
nutritional count per serving 24.3g total fat (7g saturated fat); 2065kJ (494 cal); 15.9g carbohydrate; 51.1g protein; 4.5g fibre
tip Fried noodles, also known as crispy noodles, are used in sang choy bow and chow mein. They can be found in supermarkets, usually in 50g or 100g packets, already deep-fried.

chilli fried rice with chicken and broccolini

1 tablespoon peanut oil
3 eggs, beaten lightly
1 medium brown onion (150g),
   sliced thinly
1 clove garlic, crushed
2 fresh long red chillies,
   sliced thinly
175g broccolini,
   chopped coarsely
2 cups (320g) shredded
   barbecued chicken
3 cups cold cooked white
   long-grain rice
1 tablespoon light soy sauce
1 tablespoon hoisin sauce

1 Heat about a third of the oil in wok; add half the egg, swirl wok to make a thin omelette. Remove omelette from wok; roll then cut into thin strips. Repeat process using another third of the oil and remaining egg.

2 Heat remaining oil in wok; stir-fry onion, garlic and chilli until onion softens. Add broccolini; stir-fry until tender.

3 Add remaining ingredients to wok; stir-fry until hot. Add omelette; toss gently.

preparation time 10 minutes
cooking time 15 minutes
serves 4
nutritional count per serving 15.3g total fat (3.8g saturated fat); 1881kJ (450 cal); 44.6g carbohydrate; 30.9g protein; 4.1g fibre
tips You need to cook 1 cup (200g) white long-grain rice the day before making this recipe. Spread evenly onto a tray and refrigerate overnight.
You need a large barbecued chicken, weighing approximately 900g, for this recipe.

chicken

thai basil chicken and snake bean stir-fry

800g chicken thigh fillets, sliced thinly
¼ cup (60ml) fish sauce
1 tablespoon grated palm sugar
¼ teaspoon ground white pepper
1 tablespoon peanut oil
3 cloves garlic, sliced thinly
2cm piece fresh ginger (10g), sliced thinly
½ teaspoon dried chilli flakes
250g snake beans, cut into 5cm lengths
2 medium yellow capsicums (400g), sliced thinly
⅓ cup (80ml) chinese cooking wine
⅓ cup (80ml) lemon juice
1 tablespoon dark soy sauce
½ cup loosely packed thai basil leaves

1 Combine chicken, fish sauce, sugar and pepper in large bowl, cover; refrigerate 1 hour.
2 Heat oil in wok; stir-fry chicken mixture, in batches, until just cooked through.
3 Add garlic, ginger, chilli, beans and capsicum to wok; stir-fry until beans are tender.
4 Return chicken to wok with cooking wine, juice and soy sauce; bring to the boil. Reduce heat; simmer, uncovered, 2 minutes. Remove from heat; stir in basil.

preparation time 20 minutes (plus refrigeration time)
cooking time 20 minutes
serves 4
nutritional count per serving 19.4g total fat (5.2g saturated fat); 1622kJ (388 cal); 8.6g carbohydrate; 42.4g protein; 3.3g fibre
tip Serve with fresh wide rice noodles, if you like.

chinese minced beef and spicy green beans

1 tablespoon peanut oil

800g beef mince

2 cloves garlic, crushed

3cm piece fresh ginger (15g), grated

2 long green chillies, sliced thinly lengthways

300g green beans, halved lengthways

1 medium brown onion (150g), sliced thinly

1 tablespoon lime juice

2 tablespoons light soy sauce

1 tablespoon white sugar

⅓ cup (45g) crushed roasted unsalted peanuts

1 Heat half the oil in wok; stir-fry mince, in batches, until browned and cooked.

2 Heat remaining oil in wok; stir-fry garlic, ginger, chilli, beans and onion until beans are almost tender.

3 Return mince to wok with juice, sauce and sugar; stir-fry until hot. Serve stir-fry sprinkled with nuts.

preparation time 10 minutes
cooking time 15 minutes
serves 4
nutritional count per serving 23.9g total fat (7.2g saturated fat); 1864kJ (446 cal); 9.7g carbohydrate; 46.3g protein; 3.8g fibre

beef

chilli-garlic mince with snake beans

2 cloves garlic, quartered
2 long green chillies, chopped coarsely
2 fresh small red thai chillies, chopped coarsely
1 tablespoon peanut oil
600g beef mince
150g snake beans, chopped coarsely
1 medium red capsicum (200g), sliced thinly
2 tablespoons kecap asin
¼ cup (60ml) hoisin sauce
4 green onions, sliced thickly
2 tablespoons crushed peanuts

1 Blend or process garlic and chillies until mixture is finely chopped.
2 Heat half the oil in wok; stir-fry garlic mixture until fragrant. Add mince; stir-fry, in batches, until cooked through.
3 Heat remaining oil in cleaned wok; stir-fry beans and capsicum until tender.
4 Return mince to wok with sauces and onion; stir-fry until hot. Sprinkle over nuts; serve with lime wedges, if you like.

preparation time 10 minutes
cooking time 15 minutes
serves 4
nutritional count per serving 18.6g total fat (5.6g saturated fat); 1476kJ (353 cal); 9.0g carbohydrate; 34.8g protein; 4.2g fibre
tip Kecap asin is a thick, salty dark soy sauce. It is available from Asian food stores and major supermarkets.

honey and five-spice beef with broccolini

1 teaspoon five-spice powder
4cm piece fresh ginger (20g), grated
750g beef strips
2 tablespoons peanut oil
¼ cup (60ml) dark soy sauce
2 tablespoons honey
2 teaspoons lemon juice
350g broccolini, chopped coarsely
⅓ cup (35g) walnuts, chopped coarsely
1 tablespoon toasted sesame seeds

1 Combine five-spice, ginger, beef and half the oil in large bowl. Cover; refrigerate 1 hour.
2 Heat remaining oil in wok; stir-fry beef, in batches, until browned.
3 Add sauce, honey and juice to wok; bring to the boil. Reduce heat; simmer, 2 minutes.
4 Return beef to wok with broccolini; stir-fry until broccolini is tender. Remove from heat; sprinkle with nuts and seeds.

preparation time 10 minutes (plus refrigeration time)
cooking time 15 minutes
serves 4
nutritional count per serving 28.1g total fat (6.9g saturated fat); 2077kJ (497 cal); 12.8g carbohydrate; 46.7g protein; 4.6g fibre

lamb

chilli lamb stir-fry

2 tablespoons peanut oil
500g lamb fillets, sliced thinly
4cm piece fresh ginger (20g), sliced thinly
1 large brown onion (200g), sliced thickly
1 large red capsicum (350g), sliced thickly
2 tablespoons water
1 teaspoon dried chilli flakes
2 tablespoons oyster sauce
2 tablespoons light soy sauce

1 Heat half the oil in wok; stir-fry lamb, in batches, until browned.
2 Heat remaining oil in wok; stir-fry ginger, onion and capsicum, 5 minutes.
Add the water; cook, covered, about 10 minutes or until vegetables soften.
3 Return lamb to wok with chilli and sauces; stir-fry, 2 minutes or until
heated through.

preparation time 10 minutes
cooking time 25 minutes
serves 4
nutritional count per serving 13.9g total fat (3.7g saturated fat);
1154kJ (276 cal); 8.7g carbohydrate; 28.4g protein; 1.6g fibre
tip Serve stir-fry with steamed jasmine rice, if you like.

lamb teriyaki with broccolini

1 tablespoon vegetable oil
800g lamb strips
4 green onions, chopped coarsely
3cm piece fresh ginger (15g), grated
175g broccolini, chopped coarsely
150g green beans, trimmed, halved crossways
⅓ cup (80ml) teriyaki sauce
2 tablespoons honey
2 teaspoons sesame oil
1 tablespoon toasted sesame seeds

1 Heat half the vegetable oil in wok; stir-fry lamb, in batches, until browned.
2 Heat remaining vegetable oil in wok; stir-fry onion and ginger until onion softens. Add broccolini and beans; stir-fry until vegetables are tender. Remove from wok.
3 Add sauce, honey and sesame oil to wok; bring to the boil. Boil, uncovered, about 3 minutes or until sauce thickens slightly. Return lamb and vegetables to wok; stir-fry until hot. Sprinkle with seeds.

preparation time 10 minutes
cooking time 15 minutes
serves 4
nutritional count per serving 15.9g total fat (4.3g saturated fat); 1626kJ (389 cal); 14.1g carbohydrate; 45.7g protein; 3.4g fibre
tip Serve with steamed jasmine rice, if you like.

lamb

thai lamb, eggplant and coriander

1 tablespoon peanut oil
750g lamb strips
6 baby eggplants (360g), chopped coarsely
2 fresh small red thai chillies, chopped finely
1 medium brown onion (150g), chopped coarsely
2 cloves garlic, crushed
2 tablespoons grated palm sugar
2 tablespoons lime juice
1 tablespoon fish sauce
1 tablespoon light soy sauce
1 cup loosely packed fresh coriander leaves

1 Heat half the oil in wok; stir-fry lamb, in batches, until browned.
2 Heat remaining oil in wok; stir-fry eggplant until almost tender. Add chilli, onion and garlic; stir-fry until onion softens.
3 Return lamb to wok with sugar, juice and sauces; stir-fry until hot. Remove from heat; stir two-thirds of the coriander into stir-fry, sprinkle with remaining coriander.

preparation time 10 minutes
cooking time 20 minutes
serves 4
nutritional count per serving 21.4g total fat (8.3g saturated fat); 1722kJ (412 cal); 11.7g carbohydrate; 41.9g protein; 3.2g fibre
tip Serve with steamed rice, if you like.

hoisin sweet chilli lamb and mixed vegetables

1 tablespoon peanut oil
750g lamb strips
2 cloves garlic, sliced thinly
400g packaged fresh stir-fry vegetables
⅓ cup (80ml) hoisin sauce
2 tablespoons sweet chilli sauce
2 tablespoons water

1 Heat half the oil in wok; stir-fry lamb, in batches, until cooked.
2 Heat remaining oil in wok; stir-fry garlic and vegetables until vegetables are almost tender. Return lamb to wok with sauces and the water; stir-fry until hot.

preparation time 10 minutes
cooking time 15 minutes
serves 4
nutritional count per serving 23.1g total fat (8.7g saturated fat); 1877kJ (449 cal); 17.2g carbohydrate; 41.4g protein; 4.5g fibre
tip Packaged fresh stir-fry vegetables are available from supermarkets.

lamb

cantonese lamb and peas

1 tablespoon peanut oil
800g lamb strips
1 medium brown onion (150g), sliced thinly
1 clove garlic, crushed
150g snow peas, trimmed
150g sugar snap peas, trimmed
⅔ cup (80g) frozen peas
115g baby corn, halved lengthways
1 tablespoon dark soy sauce
1 tablespoon char siu sauce
¼ cup (60ml) chicken stock
1 tablespoon cornflour
2 tablespoons lime juice

1 Heat half the oil in wok; stir-fry lamb, in batches, until browned.
2 Heat remaining oil in wok; stir-fry onion and garlic until onion softens. Add peas and corn; stir-fry until corn is almost tender.
3 Return lamb to wok with sauces and stock; stir-fry about 2 minutes or until lamb is cooked. Stir in blended cornflour and juice; stir-fry until sauce boils and thickens.

preparation time 20 minutes
cooking time 15 minutes
serves 4
nutritional count per serving 23.2g total fat (8.9g saturated fat); 1977kJ (473 cal); 16g carbohydrate; 47.6g protein; 5.4g fibre
tips Char siu sauce may also be labelled chinese barbecue sauce; it is available from Asian food stores and most major supermarkets. You can use lamb backstrap for this recipe, if you prefer, slicing it thinly before use.

fried noodles with sausage and cabbage

450g wide fresh rice noodles

2 teaspoons peanut oil

300g dried chinese sausages, sliced thickly

1 medium brown onion (150g), chopped coarsely

2 cloves garlic, crushed

100g fresh shiitake mushrooms, chopped coarsely

1 small wombok (700g), chopped coarsely

¼ cup (60ml) chicken stock

¼ cup (95g) char siu sauce

2 tablespoons lime juice

½ cup loosely packed fresh coriander leaves

¼ cup loosely packed fresh mint leaves

⅓ cup (50g) coarsely chopped roasted unsalted cashews

1 fresh long red chilli, sliced thinly

1 Place noodles in large heatproof bowl, cover with boiling water; separate with fork, drain.

2 Heat oil in wok; stir-fry sausage, onion, garlic and mushrooms until sausage is browned and vegetables are tender.

3 Add wombok to wok; stir-fry until wombok wilts. Add stock, sauce, juice and noodles; stir-fry until hot. Remove from heat; sprinkle over coriander, mint, nuts and chilli.

preparation time 25 minutes

cooking time 10 minutes

serves 4

nutritional count per serving 28.4g total fat (7.8g saturated fat); 2161kJ (517 cal); 43.6g carbohydrate; 17.6g protein; 9.8g fibre

tip Dried chinese sausages, also called lop chong, are commonly made from pork but can be made with duck liver or beef. Red-brown in colour and sweet-spicy in flavour, they are sold, dried and strung, in all Asian food stores.

pork

chiang mai pork and eggplant

3 fresh small red thai chillies, halved

6 cloves garlic, quartered

1 medium brown onion (150g), chopped coarsely

500g baby eggplants

¼ cup (60ml) peanut oil

700g pork leg steaks, sliced thinly

1 tablespoon fish sauce

1 tablespoon dark soy sauce

1 tablespoon grated palm sugar

4 purple thai shallots (100g), sliced thinly

150g snake beans, cut into 5cm lengths

1 cup loosely packed thai basil leaves

1 Blend or process chilli, garlic and onion until mixture forms a paste.

2 Quarter eggplants lengthways; slice each piece into 5cm lengths. Cook eggplant in large saucepan of boiling water until just tender; drain, pat dry.

3 Heat half the oil in wok; stir-fry eggplant, in batches, until browned lightly. Drain on absorbent paper.

4 Heat remaining oil in wok; stir-fry pork, in batches, until cooked.

5 Stir-fry garlic paste in wok about 3 minutes or until fragrant and browned lightly. Add sauces and sugar; stir-fry until sugar dissolves.

6 Add shallot and beans to wok; stir-fry until beans are tender. Return eggplant and pork to wok; stir-fry until hot. Remove from heat; sprinkle with basil.

preparation time 20 minutes
cooking time 25 minutes
serves 4
nutritional count per serving 19.3g total fat (4.1g saturated fat); 1672kJ (400 cal); 10.1g carbohydrate; 43.6g protein; 5.8g fibre
tip Thai purple shallots, also known as pink shallots or homm, are used all over South-East Asia. While good used in cooking, they also can be eaten raw in salads or deep-fried as a condiment.

quick pork fried rice

600g pork fillets, sliced thinly
1 tablespoon honey
2 tablespoons kecap manis
2 teaspoons peanut oil
2 eggs, beaten lightly
1 medium carrot (120g), cut
    into matchsticks
1 medium red capsicum
    (200g), sliced thinly
3 cups cold cooked white
    long-grain rice
8 green onions, sliced thinly
1 cup (80g) bean sprouts
2 tablespoons soy sauce
2 tablespoons char siu sauce

1 Combine pork in medium bowl with honey and kecap manis.

2 Heat half the oil in wok. Pour egg into wok; cook over medium heat, tilting pan, until almost set. Remove omelette from wok; roll tightly, slice thinly.

3 Heat remaining oil in wok; stir-fry pork, in batches, until cooked.

4 Stir-fry carrot and capsicum in wok until just tender.

5 Return half the omelette to wok with rice, pork, onion, sprouts and sauces; stir-fry until hot. Remove from heat; sprinkle with remaining omelette.

preparation time 20 minutes
cooking time 15 minutes
serves 4
nutritional count per serving
9.4g total fat (2.5g saturated fat);
2032kJ (486 cal); 54.6g carbohydrate;
42.6g protein; 4.7g fibre
tip You need to cook 1 cup (200g) of rice the day before making this recipe. Spread evenly onto a tray; refrigerate overnight.

stir-fried pork, buk choy and water chestnuts

1 tablespoon honey
1 tablespoon chinese cooking wine
1 teaspoon five-spice powder
½ teaspoon sesame oil
1 clove garlic, crushed
¼ cup (60ml) light soy sauce
2 tablespoons oyster sauce
600g pork fillets, sliced thinly
2 tablespoons peanut oil
600g baby buk choy, chopped coarsely
227g can water chestnuts, rinsed, drained, sliced thickly
½ cup (75g) unsalted roasted cashews
2 long green chillies, sliced thinly
1 tablespoon water

1 Combine honey, cooking wine, five-spice, sesame oil, garlic, 2 tablespoons of the soy sauce, 1 tablespoon of the oyster sauce and pork in large bowl. Cover; refrigerate 3 hours or overnight.
2 Stir-fry pork in oiled wok, in batches, until browned.
3 Heat peanut oil in wok; stir-fry buk choy, water chestnuts, nuts and chilli until tender.
4 Return pork to wok with remaining soy and oyster sauces and the water; stir-fry until hot.

preparation time 15 minutes (plus refrigeration time)
cooking time 15 minutes
serves 4
nutritional count per serving 23g total fat (4.5g saturated fat); 1827kJ (437 cal); 15.8g carbohydrate; 39.1g protein; 4.1g fibre

char siu pork, corn and choy sum

2 tablespoons peanut oil
600g pork fillets, sliced thinly
2 medium brown onions (300g), cut into thin wedges
230g baby corn
300g choy sum, trimmed, chopped coarsely
2 tablespoons char siu sauce
2 teaspoons light soy sauce
2 teaspoons lime juice
1 fresh long red chilli, sliced thinly

1   Heat half the oil in wok; stir-fry pork, in batches, until browned.
2   Heat remaining oil in wok; stir-fry onion and corn until onion softens.
3   Return pork to wok with choy sum, sauces and juice; stir-fry until hot.
Sprinkle with chilli.

preparation time 10 minutes
cooking time 15 minutes
serves 4
nutritional count per serving 14g total fat (3g saturated fat);
1513kJ (362 cal); 18.4g carbohydrate; 37.5g protein; 5.7g fibre

javanese stir-fried pork and rice noodles

450g fresh wide rice noodles
1 tablespoon vegetable oil
500g pork mince
2 cloves garlic, crushed
1 tablespoon sambal oelek
4 green onions, sliced thinly
⅓ cup (80ml) kecap manis
2 baby buk choy (300g), leaves separated
1 cup loosely packed fresh coriander leaves

1 Place noodles in large heatproof bowl, cover with boiling water; separate with fork, drain.
2 Heat oil in wok; stir-fry pork until browned and cooked through. Add garlic, sambal, onion and 1 tablespoon of the kecap manis; stir-fry 1 minute.
3 Add noodles, remaining kecap manis and buk choy to wok; stir-fry until hot. Sprinkle with coriander.

preparation time 10 minutes
cooking time 15 minutes
serves 4
nutritional count per serving 14.5g total fat (3.8g saturated fat); 1927kJ (461 cal); 49g carbohydrate; 31.1g protein; 2.8g fibre

sichuan eggplant, almond and wombok stir-fry

⅓ cup (55g) blanched almonds, halved
1 tablespoon peanut oil
1 medium brown onion (150g), chopped coarsely
2 cloves garlic, crushed
1 fresh small red thai chilli, chopped finely
12 baby eggplants (720g), sliced thickly
150g snake beans, trimmed, chopped coarsely
1 small wombok (700g), trimmed, chopped coarsely
2 teaspoons sichuan peppercorns, crushed coarsely
¼ cup (60ml) vegetable stock
2 tablespoons hoisin sauce
1 tablespoon dark soy sauce
1 tablespoon red wine vinegar
½ cup loosely packed thai basil leaves
1 fresh long red chilli, sliced thinly

1 Stir-fry nuts in heated wok until browned lightly; remove from wok.
2 Heat oil in wok; stir-fry onion, garlic and chopped chilli until onion softens. Add eggplant and beans; stir-fry until tender. Add wombok; stir-fry until wilted.
3 Add pepper, stock, sauces and vinegar to wok; stir-fry until hot. Remove from heat; stir in basil. Serve sprinkled with nuts and sliced chilli.

preparation time 15 minutes
cooking time 20 minutes
serves 4
nutritional count per serving 13.6g total fat (1.4g saturated fat); 982kJ (235cal); 13.9g carbohydrate; 9.3g protein; 10.7g fibre
tip Serve with stir-fried hokkien noodles, if you like.

tofu, cashew and vegie stir-fry

1 tablespoon vegetable oil
1 fresh long red chilli, sliced thinly
500g packaged fresh stir-fry vegetables
400g packaged marinated tofu pieces, chopped coarsely
½ cup (75g) roasted unsalted cashews
⅓ cup (80ml) hoisin sauce
1 tablespoon lime juice

1 Heat oil in wok; stir-fry chilli, vegetables, tofu and nuts until vegetables are just tender.
2 Add sauce and juice; stir-fry until hot.

preparation time 5 minutes
cooking time 10 minutes
serves 4
nutritional count per serving 22.6g total fat (3.4g saturated fat); 1563kJ (374 cal); 20.9g carbohydrate; 18.2g protein; 8.4g fibre
tips We used cryovac-packed ready-to-serve sweet chilli tofu, available from many supermarkets and Asian food stores.
Packaged fresh stir-fry vegetables are available from supermarkets.

coconut rice with capsicum and coriander

½ cup (40g) shredded
  coconut
2 tablespoons vegetable oil
2 teaspoons chilli oil
1 medium brown onion (150g),
  chopped coarsely
1 medium red capsicum
  (200g), chopped coarsely
3 cloves garlic, crushed
3cm piece fresh ginger (15g),
  grated
1½ cups (300g) calrose rice
1½ cups (375ml) vegetable
  stock
1 cup (250ml) water
140ml can coconut milk
3 green onions, chopped
  coarsely
¼ cup coarsely chopped
  fresh coriander
¼ cup (60ml) lemon juice
¼ cup fresh coriander leaves

1 Heat wok, add coconut; stir constantly until browned lightly. Remove from wok.
2 Heat oils in wok; stir-fry brown onion, capsicum, garlic and ginger until onion softens.
3 Add rice to wok; stir-fry 2 minutes. Add stock, the water and coconut milk; simmer, covered, about 20 minutes or until liquid is absorbed and rice is tender.
4 Remove from heat; stir in green onion, chopped coriander, juice and half the coconut. Sprinkle with remaining coconut and coriander leaves to serve.

preparation time 15 minutes
cooking time 20 minutes
serves 4
nutritional count per serving 26.2g total fat (13.9g saturated fat); 2282kJ (546 cal); 66.4g carbohydrate; 9g protein; 4.5g fibre
tip You could use chicken stock, if you prefer. Calrose rice is a medium-grain rice that is extremely versatile; you can substitute short- or long-grain rice, if necessary.

sweet and sour vegetables with fried tofu

1 tablespoon peanut oil
1 medium red onion (170g), sliced thinly
1 fresh long red chilli, sliced thinly
250g button mushrooms, quartered
575g jar sweet and sour sauce
200g packet fried tofu, cut into 2cm cubes
150g snow peas, trimmed
115g baby corn, halved lengthways
230g can sliced bamboo shoots, rinsed, drained
½ cup (75g) roasted unsalted cashews

1   Heat oil in wok; stir-fry onion, chilli and mushrooms until onion softens.
2   Add sauce; bring to the boil. Add tofu, peas, corn and bamboo shoots; stir-fry until hot. Remove from heat; sprinkle with nuts.

preparation time 10 minutes
cooking time 10 minutes
serves 4
nutritional count per serving 19.9g total fat (3.6g saturated fat); 2354kJ (563 cal); 79.6g carbohydrate; 13.8g protein; 8.5g fibre
tip We used a packaged fried tofu, which can be bought from many supermarkets. If you prefer to do it yourself, shallow-fry cubes of drained firm silken tofu in vegetable oil until just browned; drain well before tossing with vegetables.

sweet soy fried noodles

Known as "pad sieu" this traditional Thai dish is similar to the famous "pad thai", but uses kecap manis, a thick, sweet soy sauce, to give it its special flavour.

450g fresh wide rice noodles
1 tablespoon peanut oil
3 cloves garlic, sliced thinly
2 eggs, beaten lightly
280g gai lan, chopped
    coarsely
200g snake beans, cut into
    5cm lengths
⅓ cup (80ml) kecap manis
2 tablespoons light soy sauce
½ teaspoon dried chilli flakes
350g packet fried tofu, cut
    into 2cm cubes
4 green onions, sliced thinly
¾ cup loosely packed
    thai basil leaves

1 Place noodles in large heatproof bowl, cover with boiling water; separate with fork, drain.
2 Heat oil in wok; stir-fry garlic until fragrant. Add egg; stir-fry until set. Add vegetables, sauces and chilli; stir-fry until vegetables are tender. Add noodles, tofu, onion and basil; stir-fry until hot.

preparation time 15 minutes
cooking time 20 minutes
serves 4
nutritional count per serving 18.2g total fat (4g saturated fat); 2036kJ (487 cal); 55.4g carbohydrate; 20.1g protein; 9.8g fibre
tip We used a packaged fried tofu available from many supermarkets. If you prefer to do it yourself, simply shallow-fry cubes of drained firm silken tofu in vegetable oil until just browned; drain well before tossing with vegetables.

glossary

bamboo shoots tender, pale yellow, edible first-growth of the bamboo plant; drain and rinse before use. Available in cans from supermarkets and Asian food stores.

basil an aromatic herb; the most commonly used is sweet, or common, basil.

thai has smallish leaves and sweet licorice/aniseed taste. Available in Asian food stores and greengrocers.

beans

bean sprouts also known as bean shoots; tender new growths of assorted beans and seeds. The most readily available are mung bean, soy bean, alfalfa and snow pea sprouts.

snake long (about 40cm), thin, round, fresh green beans; Asian in origin, with a taste similar to green or french beans. Also known as yard-long beans because of their (pre-metric) length.

broccolini a cross between broccoli and chinese kale; milder and sweeter than broccoli. Each long stem is topped by a loose floret that closely resembles broccoli; from floret to stem, broccolini is completely edible.

buk choy also known as bok choy, pak choi, chinese white cabbage or chinese chard; has a fresh, mild mustard taste. Baby buk choy, also known as shanghai bok choy, is smaller and more tender.

capsicum also known as bell pepper or, simply, pepper. Discard membranes and seeds before use.

cardamom purchase in pod, seed or ground form. Has an aromatic, sweetly rich flavour; is one of the world's most expensive spices.

chilli available in many types and sizes. Use rubber gloves when seeding and chopping fresh chillies as they can burn your skin. Removing seeds and membranes lessens the heat level.

flakes, dried deep-red dehydrated extremely fine slices and whole seeds.

green any unripened chilli; also some varieties that are ripe when green.

long red available fresh and dried; a generic term used for any moderately hot, long, (6cm-8cm) thin chilli.

red thai small, hot and bright red in colour.

chinese cooking wine also known as chinese rice wine or hao hsing; made from fermented rice, wheat, sugar and salt. Found in Asian food shops; if you can't find it, replace it with mirin or sherry.

choy sum also known as pakaukeo or flowering cabbage; has long stems, light green leaves and yellow flowers. Is eaten, stir-fried, stems and all.

coriander also known as pak chee, cilantro or chinese parsley; bright-green-leafed herb with a pungent flavour.

cornflour also known as cornstarch.

cucumber, telegraph also known as the european or burpless cucumber; slender and long, its thin dark-green skin has shallow ridges running down its length.

eggplant, baby also known as finger or japanese eggplant; a very small, slender eggplant.

five-spice powder a mix of ground cinnamon, cloves, star anise, sichuan pepper and fennel seeds.

gai lan also known as chinese broccoli, gai larn, kanah, gai lum, chinese kale; appreciated more for its stems than its coarse leaves.

golden syrup a by-product of refined sugarcane; pure maple syrup or honey can be substituted.

kecap manis see sauces.

mince also known as ground meat.

mushrooms

enoki clumps of long, spaghetti-like stems with tiny, snowy white caps.

oyster also known as abalone; grey-white mushroom shaped like a fan. Prized for their smooth texture and subtle, oyster-like flavour.

shiitake when fresh are also known as golden oak, forest, or chinese black mushrooms. Are large and meaty, and have the earthiness and taste of wild mushrooms.

noodles

fresh rice chewy, pure white noodle; also known as ho fun, khao pun, sen yau, pho or kway tiau.

fried also known as crispy noodles. Deep-fried noodles found in supermarkets, in 50g or 100g packets.

hokkien also known as stir-fry noodles; fresh wheat noodles resembling thick, yellow-brown spaghetti.

onions

green also known as scallion or, incorrectly, shallot; an immature onion picked before the bulb has formed, having a long, bright-green edible stalk.

red also known as spanish, red spanish or bermuda onion; a sweet-flavoured, large, purple-red onion.

shallots also called french shallots, golden shallots or eschalots.

thai purple shallots also known as pink shallots or homm. They grow in multiple-clove bulbs, like garlic, and are intensely flavoured.

prawns known as shrimp.

sambal oelek (also ulek or olek) Indonesian in origin; a salty paste made from ground chillies and vinegar.

sauces

char siu chinese barbecue sauce made from sugar, water, salt, fermented soya bean paste, honey, soy sauce, malt syrup and spices. It can be found at most supermarkets.

fish also called nam pla or nuoc nam; made from pulverised salted fermented fish, most often anchovies. Has a pungent smell and strong taste; use sparingly.

hoisin made from salted fermented soya beans, onions and garlic; used as a marinade or baste.

oyster Asian in origin, this rich, brown sauce is made from oysters and their brine, cooked with salt and soy sauce, and thickened with starches.

plum a thick, sweet and sour dipping sauce made from plums, vinegar, sugar, chillies and spices.

soy made from fermented soy beans. Several variations are available in supermarkets and Asian food stores. *Dark soy* is deep brown, almost black in colour; rich, with a thicker consistency than other types. Pungent but not particularly salty. *Kecap manis* is a dark, thick sweet soy sauce; the sweetness is derived from the addition of either molasses or palm sugar when brewed. *Light soy* has a thin consistency and is the saltiest tasting. Not to be confused with salt-reduced or low-sodium soy sauces.

sweet chilli a fairly mild sauce made from red chillies, sugar, garlic and vinegar.

teriyaki a blend of soy sauce, wine, vinegar and spices.

vegetarian mushroom oyster a "vegetarian" oyster sauce made from blended oyster mushrooms and soy.

sugar

palm also known as jaggery or gula melaka; made from the sap of the sugar palm tree. Light brown to dark-brown in colour and usually sold in rock-hard cakes; if unavailable, substitute it with brown sugar.

white coarse, granulated table sugar, also known as crystal sugar.

vinegar, red wine based on fermented red wine.

water chestnuts resembles a chestnut in appearance, hence the English name. Small brown tubers with a crisp, white, nutty-tasting flesh. Canned water chestnuts can be kept about a month, once opened, under refrigeration.

wombok also known as peking cabbage, chinese cabbage or petsai. Elongated in shape with pale green, crinkly leaves, this is the most common cabbage in South-East Asian cooking.

conversion chart

MEASURES

One Australian metric measuring cup holds approximately 250ml, one Australian metric tablespoon holds 20ml, one Australian metric teaspoon holds 5ml.

The difference between one country's measuring cups and another's is within a 2- or 3-teaspoon variance, and will not affect your cooking results. North America, New Zealand and the United Kingdom use a 15ml tablespoon. All cup and spoon measurements are level. The most accurate way of measuring dry ingredients is to weigh them. When measuring liquids, use a clear glass or plastic jug with metric markings.

We use large eggs with an average weight of 60g.

DRY MEASURES

METRIC	IMPERIAL
15g	½oz
30g	1oz
60g	2oz
90g	3oz
125g	4oz (¼lb)
155g	5oz
185g	6oz
220g	7oz
250g	8oz (½lb)
280g	9oz
315g	10oz
345g	11oz
375g	12oz (¾lb)
410g	13oz
440g	14oz
470g	15oz
500g	16oz (1lb)
750g	24oz (1½lb)
1kg	32oz (2lb)

LIQUID MEASURES

METRIC	IMPERIAL
30ml	1 fluid oz
60ml	2 fluid oz
100ml	3 fluid oz
125ml	4 fluid oz
150ml	5 fluid oz (¼ pint/1 gill)
190ml	6 fluid oz
250ml	8 fluid oz
300ml	10 fluid oz (½ pint)
500ml	16 fluid oz
600ml	20 fluid oz (1 pint)
1000ml (1 litre)	1¾ pints

LENGTH MEASURES

METRIC	IMPERIAL
3mm	⅛in
6mm	¼in
1cm	½in
2cm	¾in
2.5cm	1in
5cm	2in
6cm	2½in
8cm	3in
10cm	4in
13cm	5in
15cm	6in
18cm	7in
20cm	8in
23cm	9in
25cm	10in
28cm	11in
30cm	12in (1ft)

OVEN TEMPERATURES

These oven temperatures are only a guide for conventional ovens. For fan-forced ovens, check the manufacturer's manual.

	°C (CELSIUS)	°F (FAHRENHEIT)	GAS MARK
Very slow	120	250	½
Slow	150	275-300	1-2
Moderately slow	160	325	3
Moderate	180	350-375	4-5
Moderately hot	200	400	6
Hot	220	425-450	7-8
Very hot	240	475	9

index

TEST KITCHEN
Food director Pamela Clark
Recipe editor Louise Patniotis
Nutritional information Belinda Farlow

ACP BOOKS
General manager Christine Whiston
Editorial director Susan Tomnay
Creative director Hieu Chi Nguyen
Designer Hannah Blackmore
Senior editor Wendy Bryant
Director of sales Brian Cearnes
Marketing manager Bridget Cody
Business analyst Rebecca Varela
Operations manager David Scotto
Production manager Victoria Jefferys
International rights enquiries Laura Bamford
lbamford@acpuk.com

ACP Books are published by ACP Magazines
a division of PBL Media Pty Limited
Publishing director, Women's lifestyle Pat Ingram
Director of sales, Women's lifestyle Lynette Phillips
Commercial manager, Women's lifestyle Seymour Cohen
Marketing director, Women's lifestyle Matthew Dominello
Public relations manager, Women's lifestyle Hannah Deveraux
Creative director, Events, Women's lifestyle Luke Bonnano
Research Director, Women's lifestyle Justin Stone
PBL Media, Chief Executive Officer Ian Law

Cover Char sui pork, corn & choy sum, page 47
Photographer Rob Palmer
Stylist Michaela le Compte
Food preparation Angela Muscat

Produced by ACP Books, Sydney.
Published by ACP Books,
a division of ACP Magazines Ltd,
54 Park St, Sydney; GPO Box 4088,
Sydney, NSW 2001
phone (02) 9282 8618 fax (02) 9267 9438.
acpbooks@acpmagazines.com.au
www.acpbooks.com.au
Printed by Dai Nippon in Korea.
Australia Distributed by Network Services,
phone +61 2 9282 8777 fax +61 2 9264 3278
networkweb@networkservicescompany.com.au
United Kingdom Distributed by Australian
Consolidated Press (UK),
phone (01604) 642 200 fax (01604) 642 300
books@acpuk.com
New Zealand Distributed by Netlink Distribution
Company, phone (9) 366 9966 ask@ndc.co.nz
South Africa Distributed by PSD Promotions,
phone (27 11) 392 6065/6/7 fax (27 11) 392
6079/80 orders@psdprom.co.za
Canada Distributed by Publishers Group Canada
phone (800) 663 5714 fax (800) 565 3770
service@raincoast.com

Title: Stir-fried / food director Pamela Clark.
ISBN: 9781863968874 (pbk.)
Notes: Includes index.
Subjects: Stir frying.
Other Authors/Contributors: Clark, Pamela.
Dewey Number: 641.774
© ACP Magazines Ltd 2009
ABN 18 053 273 546
This publication is copyright. No part of it may be
reproduced or transmitted in any form without
the written permission of the publishers.
Send recipe enquiries to:
recipeenquiries@acpmagazines.com.au